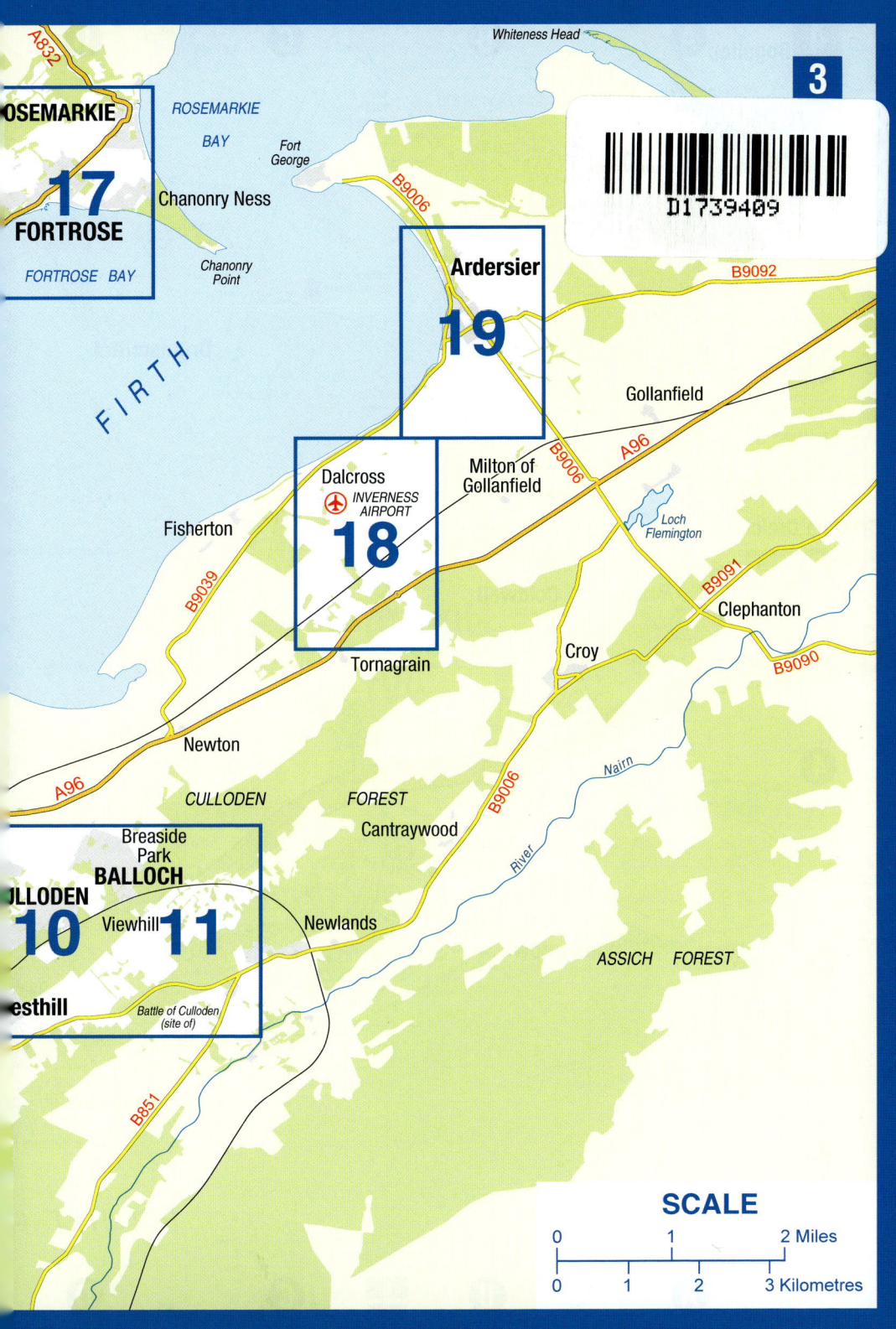

A-Z INVERNESS

CONTENTS

Key to Map Pages	2-3
Map Pages	4-19
Large Scale City Centre	20

Index to Streets, Towns, Villages, Stations, Hospitals etc. and selected Places of Interest — 21-28

REFERENCE

A Road	A862
B Road	B865
Dual Carriageway	
One-way Street	
Traffic flow on A Roads is also indicated by a heavy line on the driver's left.	
Road Under Construction	
Opening dates are correct at the time of publication	
Proposed Road	
Restricted Access	
Pedestrianized Road	
Track	
Footpath	
Residential Walkway	
Railway	Station Tunnel Level Crossing
Built-up Area	MILL ST.
Posttown Boundary	
Postcode Boundary (within posttown)	
Map Continuation	8 Large Scale City Centre 20

Airport	✈
Car Park (selected)	P
Church or Chapel	†
Cycleway (selected)	🚲
Fire Station	■
Hospital	H
House Numbers (A & B Roads only)	43 8
Information Centre	i
National Grid Reference	265
Police Station	▲
Post Office	★
Toilet: without facilities for the Disabled	▽
with facilities for the Disabled	▽
Viewpoint	✳✸
Educational Establishment	▮
Hospital or Healthcare Building	▮
Industrial Building	▮
Leisure or Recreational Facility	▮
Place of Interest	▮
Public Building	▮
Shopping Centre or Market	▮
Other Selected Buildings	▮

SCALE

Map Pages 4-19 1:15,840	Map Page 20 1:7,920
0 ¼ ½ Mile	0 ⅛ ¼ Mile
0 250 500 750 Metres	0 100 200 300 Metres
4 inches (10.16cm) to 1 Mile 6.31cm to 1Km	8 inches (20.32cm) to 1 Mile 12.63cm to 1Km

Copyright of Geographers' A-Z Map Company Limited

Fairfield Road, Borough Green, Sevenoaks, Kent TN15 8PP
Telephone: 01732 781000 (Enquiries & Trade Sales)
01732 783422 (Retail Sales)

www.az.co.uk

Copyright © Geographers' A-Z Map Co. Ltd.

EDITION 4 2013

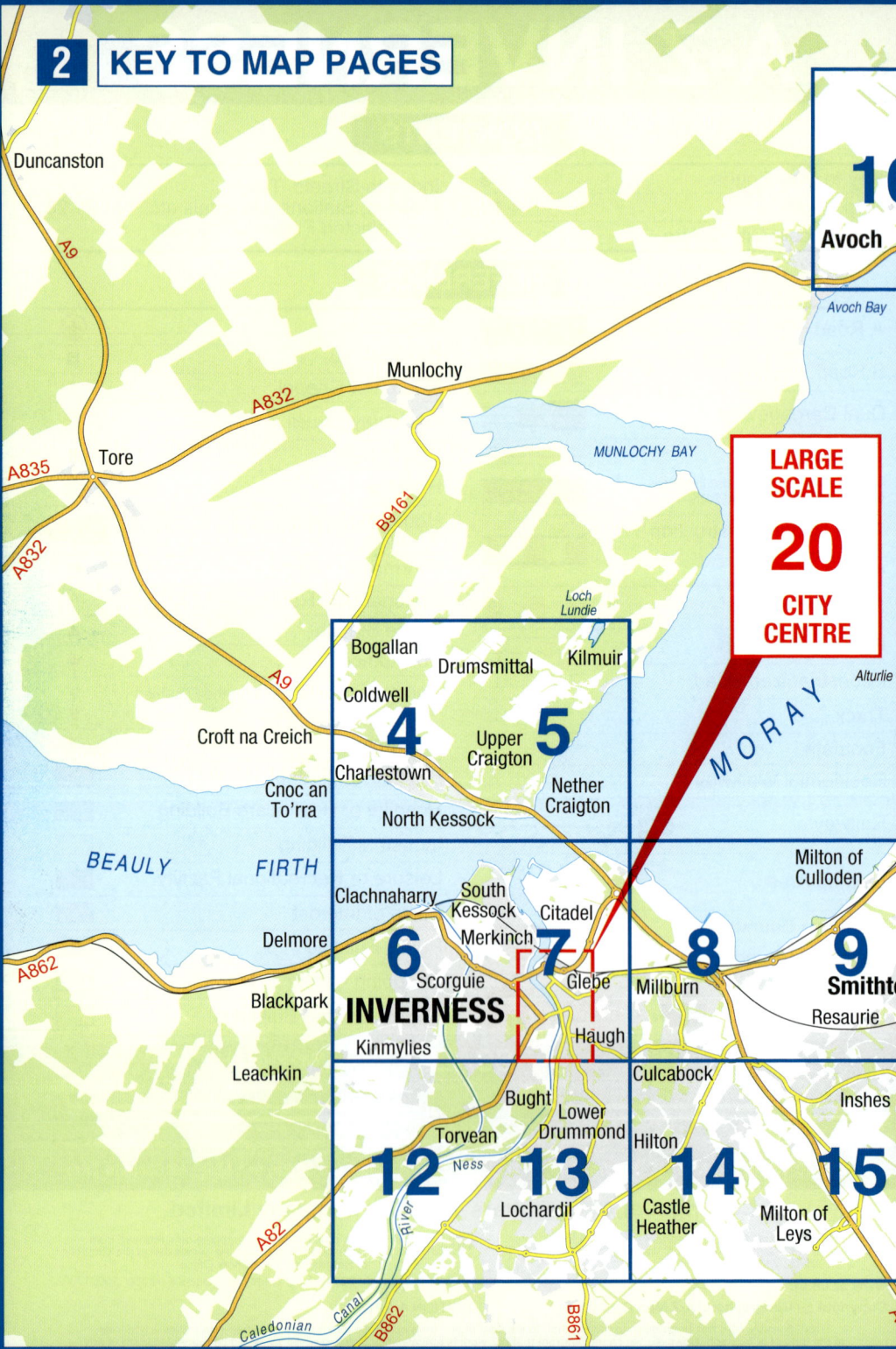

Duncanston

A9

Munlochy

A832

Tore

A835

A832

A9

B9161

MUNLOCHY BAY

Loch
Lundie

16

Avoch

Avoch Bay

**LARGE
SCALE**

20

**CITY
CENTRE**

Bogallan

Drumsmittal

Kilmuir

Coldwell

4

Upper
Craigton

5

Croft na Creich

Charlestown

Nether
Craigton

Cnoc an
To'rra

North Kessock

M O R A Y

Alturlie P

B E A U L Y   F I R T H

Milton of
Culloden

Clachnaharry

South
Kessock

Citadel

A862

Delmore

Merkinch

6

7

Glebe

8

9

Millburn

Smithto

Scorguie

Blackpark

INVERNESS

Resaurie

Kinmylies

Haugh

Leachkin

Culcabock

Inshes

Bught

Lower
Drummond

Hilton

Torvean

12

Ness

13

14

15

A82

River

Lochardil

Castle
Heather

Milton of
Leys

Caledonian   Canal

B862

B861

E   66   **F**   Creag a' Chaisteil   **G**   67   Pitlundie   **H**   Taindore Wood   **5**

Mains of
Drynie

Reservoir
(covered)

Craigieholm

Loch
Lundie

1

Loch
na Girra

Viewbank

Drynie
Lodge

850

Black Wood

New Drynie
Ho.

Letter
Kilmuir

2

Kilmuir

Culish

Craigbreck
Farm

Fearnann
nan Gras

Kilmuir Hill

3

ORD   HILL

Ord Hill
Hill Fort

49

Orienteering
Course

Boat House

Craigduff

Croft Downie

4

Windsong

Upper
Craigton

Craighill

Boat House

5

Nether
Craigton

MORAY   FIRTH

CRAIGTON
POINT

48

Dolphin
& Seal
Cen.

OLD CRAIGTON RD.

ST. POINT

ROAD

KESSOCK

6

Lifeboat
Station

Longman Beacon

A9

BRIDGE

E   66   **F**   **7**   **G**   LONGMAN
POINT   67   **H**

Inverness Caledonian

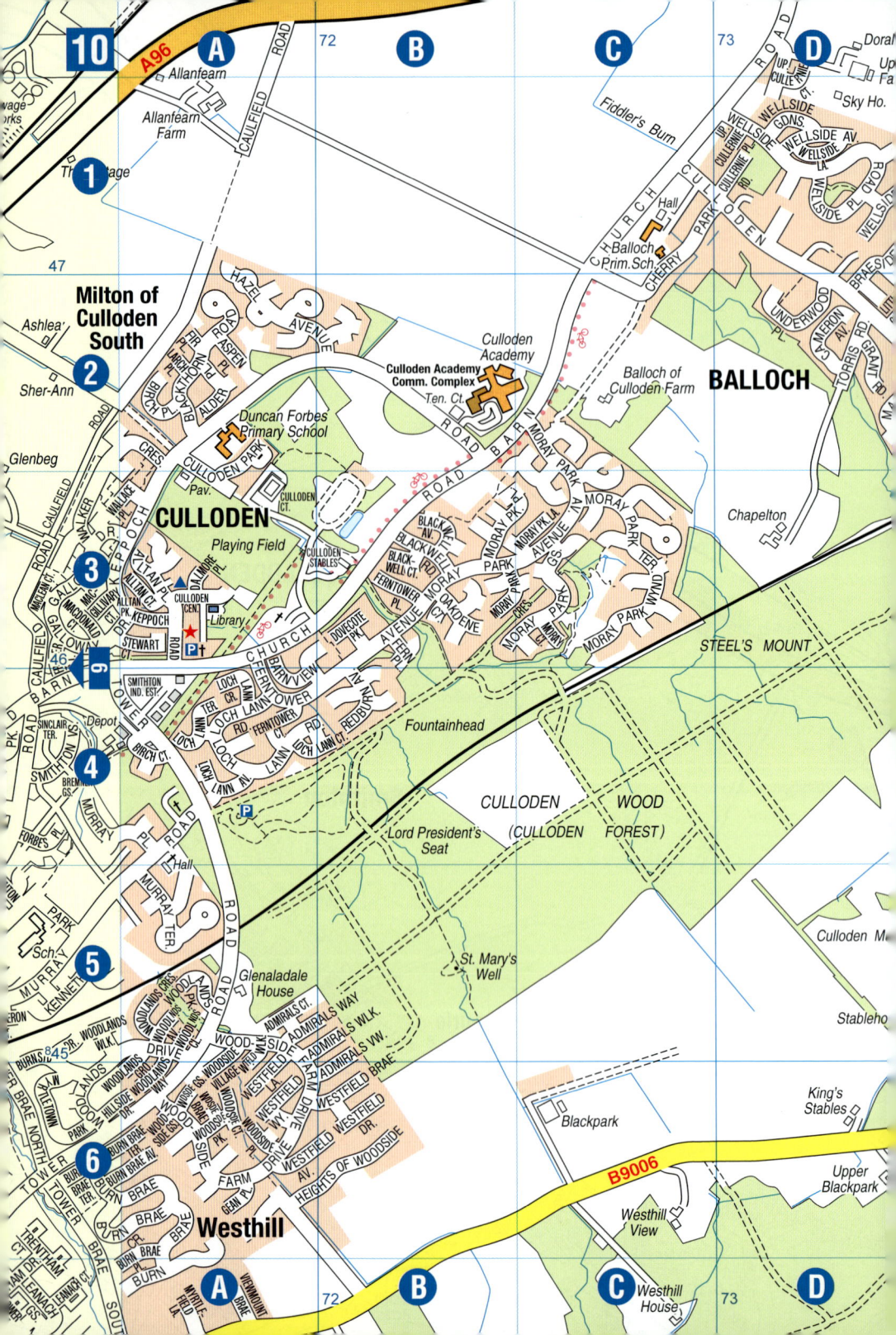

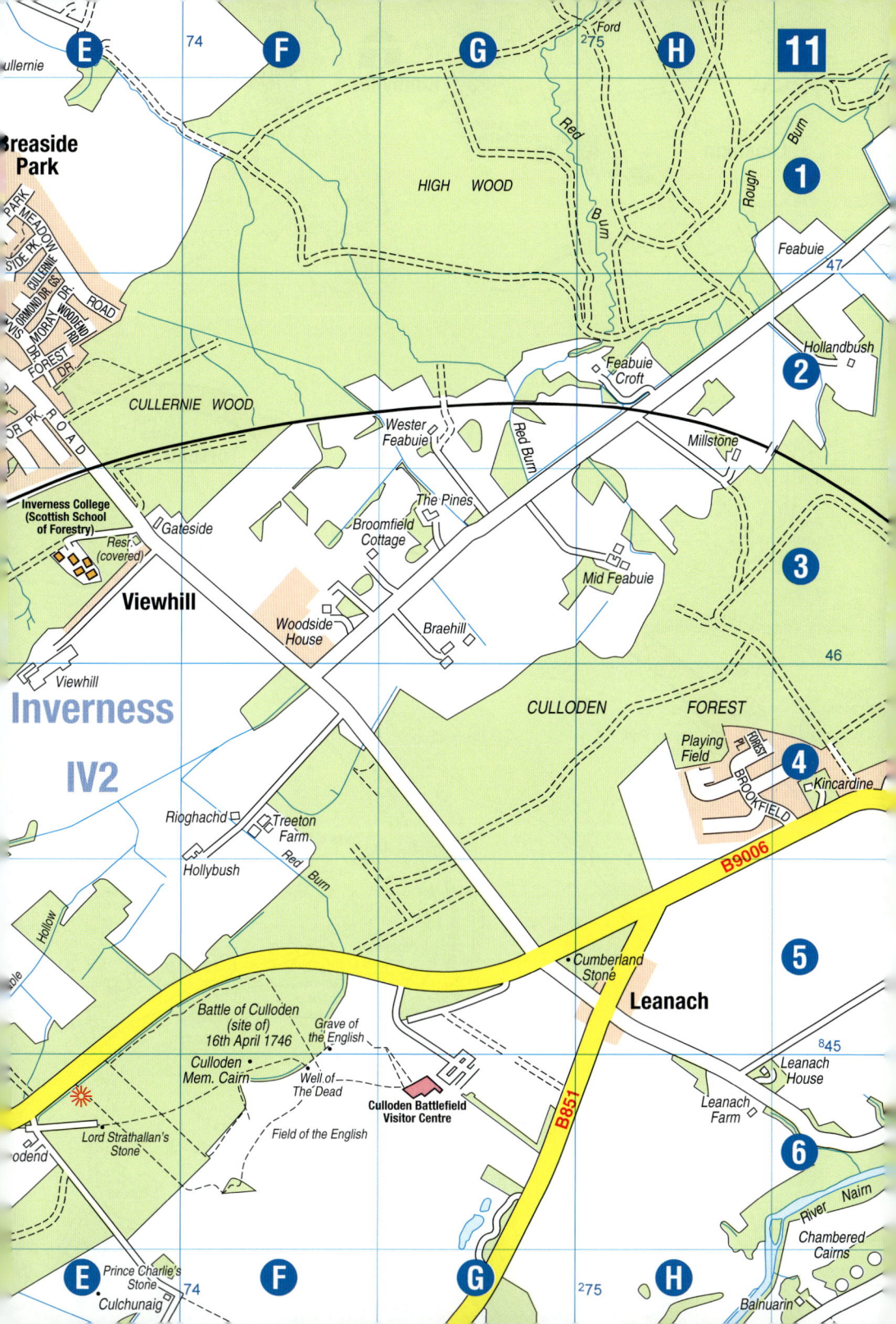

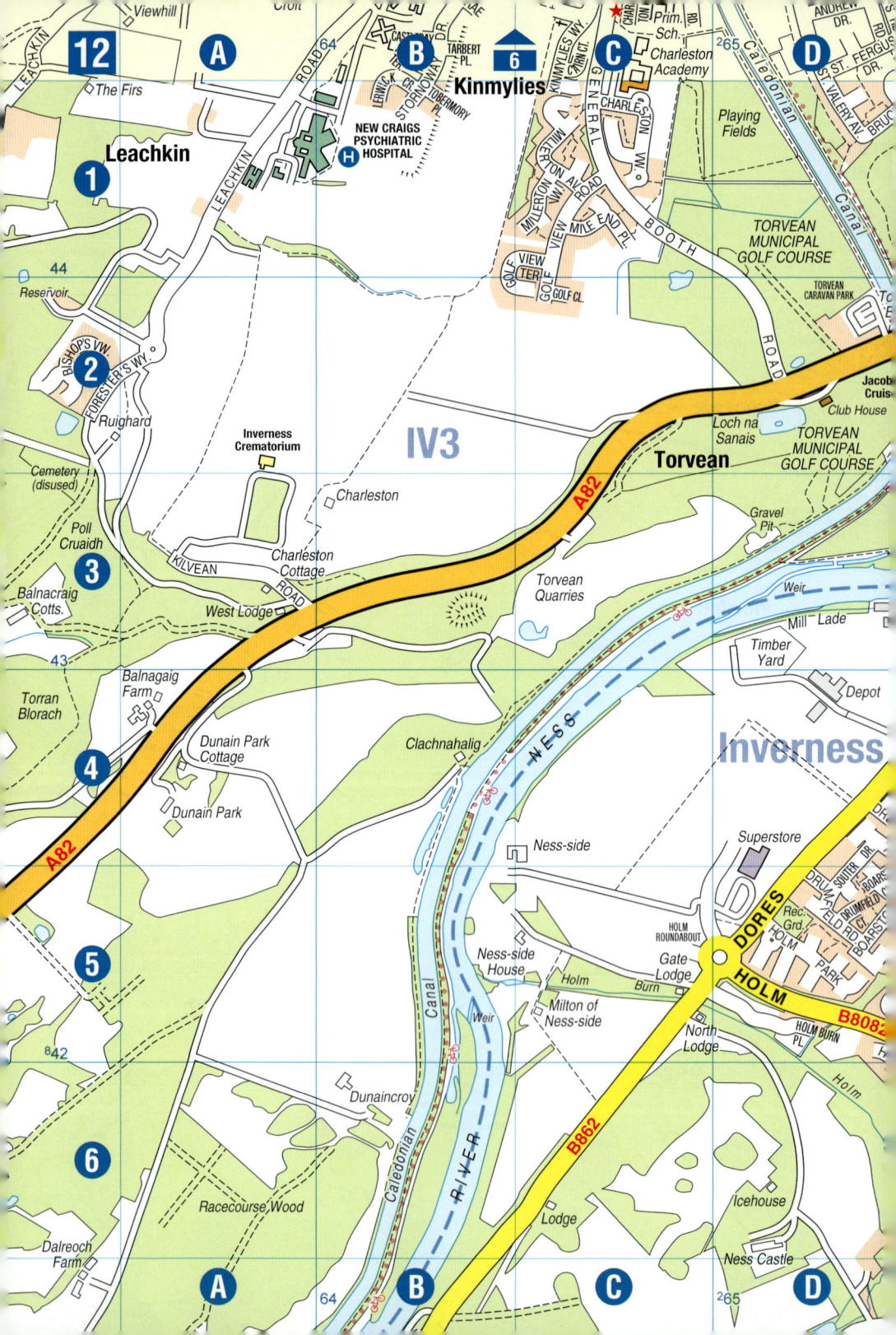

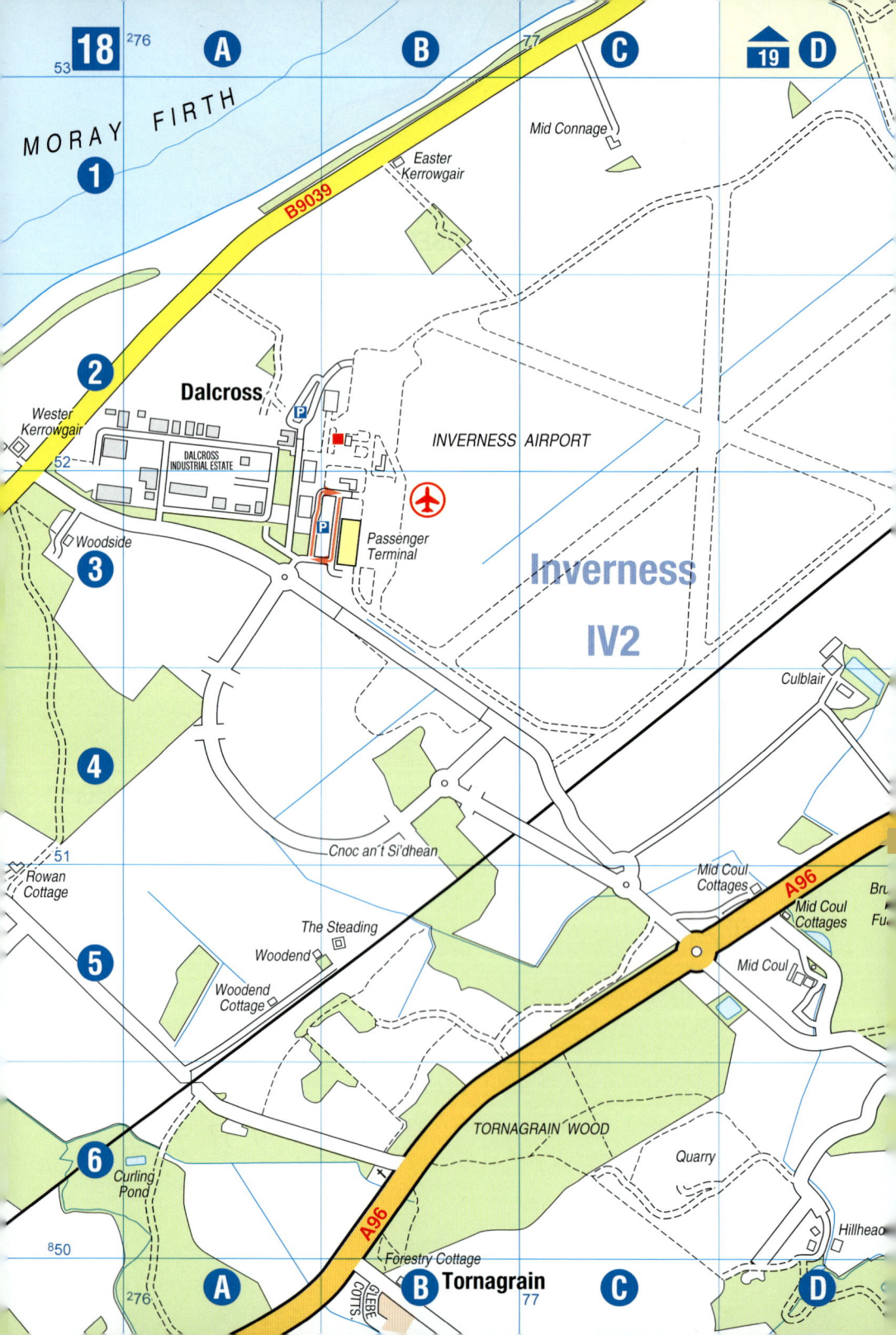

18 276
53

A

B
77

C

19 D

MORAY FIRTH

1

B9039

Easter
Kerrowgair

Mid Connage

2

Dalcross

P

Wester
Kerrowgair

52

DALCROSS
INDUSTRIAL ESTATE

P

INVERNESS AIRPORT

Woodside

3

P

Passenger
Terminal

Inverness

IV2

Culblair

4

51

Rowan
Cottage

Cnoc an't Si'dhean

Mid Coul
Cottages

A96

Bru
Fu

Mid Coul
Cottages

The Steading

Woodend

5

Woodend
Cottage

Mid Coul

6

Curling
Pond

TORNAGRAIN WOOD

Quarry

Hillhea

850

276

A

GLEBE
COTTS

B Tornagrain
77

A96

Forestry Cottage

C

D

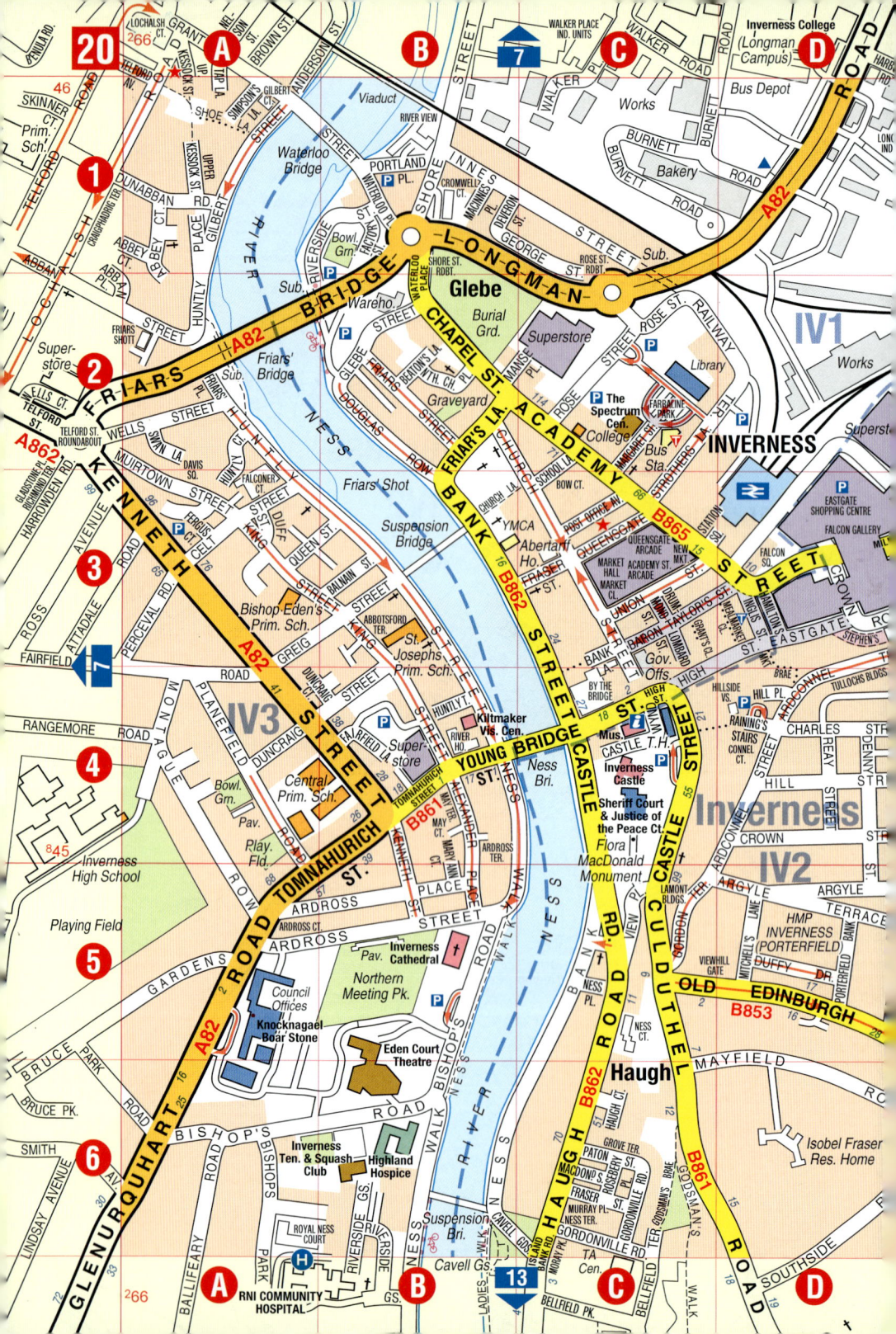

INDEX

Including Streets, Places & Areas, Hospitals etc., Industrial Estates, Selected Flats & Walkways, Stations and Selected Places of Interest.

HOW TO USE THIS INDEX

1. Each street name is followed by its Postcode District, then by its Locality abbreviation(s) and then by its map reference; e.g. **Annfield Rd.** IV2: Inve . . . .6H **7** is in the IV2 Postcode District and the Inverness Locality and is to be found in square 6H on page **7**. The page number is shown in bold type.

2. A strict alphabetical order is followed in which Av., Rd., St., etc. (though abbreviated) are read in full and as part of the street name; e.g. **King St.** appears after **Kingsmills Rd.** but before **Kingsview Ter.**

3. Streets and a selection of flats and walkways that cannot be shown on the mapping, appear in the index with the thoroughfare to which they are connected shown in brackets; e.g. **Anderson Ct.** *IV3: Inve* . . . .3F **7** *(off Madras St.)*

4. Addresses that are in more than one part are referred to as not continuous.

5. Places and areas are shown in the index in **BLUE TYPE** and the map reference is to the actual map square in which the town centre or area is located and not to the place name shown on the map; e.g. **FORTROSE** 3F **17**

6. An example of a selected place of interest is **Groam House Mus.** 1H **17**

7. An example of a station is **Inverness Station (Rail)** 3D **20** (4G **7**)

8. An example of a Hospital, Hospice or selected Healthcare facility is **RAIGMORE HOSPITAL** 6C **8**

9. Map references for entries that appear on large scale page **20** are shown first, with small scale map references shown in brackets; e.g. **Academy St.** IV1: Inve 2C **20** (4G **7**)

GENERAL ABBREVIATIONS

Arc. : Arcade	**Fld.** : Field	**Pl.** : Place
Av. : Avenue	**Gdns.** : Gardens	**Rd.** : Road
Bri. : Bridge	**Ga.** : Gate	**Rdbt.** : Roundabout
Bldgs. : Buildings	**Grn.** : Green	**Shop.** : Shopping
Bus. : Business	**Gro.** : Grove	**Sth.** : South
Cen. : Centre	**Ho.** : House	**Sq.** : Square
Chu. : Church	**Ind.** : Industrial	**St.** : Street
Circ. : Circle	**Info.** : Information	**Ter.** : Terrace
Cir. : Circus	**La.** : Lane	**Up.** : Upper
Cl. : Close	**Lit.** : Little	**Vw.** : View
Cotts. : Cottages	**Lwr.** : Lower	**Vs.** : Villas
Ct. : Court	**Mdws.** : Meadows	**Vis.** : Visitors
Cres. : Crescent	**M.** : Mews	**Wlk.** : Walk
Dr. : Drive	**Mus.** : Museum	**W.** : West
E. : East	**Nth.** : North	
Est. : Estate	**Pk.** : Park	

LOCALITY ABBREVIATIONS

All : **Allanfearn**	Culd : **Culduthel**	Leac : **Leachkin**
Ard : **Ardersier**	Cull : **Culloden**	Milt C : **Milton of Culloden**
Avo : **Avoch**	Cull M : **Culloden Moor**	Milt L : **Milton of Leys**
Ball : **Balloch**	Dal : **Dalcross**	N Kes : **North Kessock**
Cas H : **Castle Heather**	Del : **Delmore**	Rose : **Rosemarkie**
Char : **Charlestown**	Drum : **Drumsmittal**	Smith : **Smithton**
Clac : **Clachnaharry**	Fort : **Fortrose**	Torn : **Tornagrain**
Crad : **Cradlehall**	Insh : **Inshes**	West : **Westhill**
Craig D : **Craig Dunain**	Inve : **Inverness**	

A

	Academy St. Arc. IV1: Inve 3C **20**	Alexander Ct. IV10: Fort 3F **17**
	Achvraid Rd. IV2: Inve 4F **13**	Alexander Pl.
Abban Pl. IV3: Inve 2A **20** (4E **7**)	Admirals Ct. IV2: West 5A **10**	IV3: Inve 4B **20** (5F **7**)
Abban St. IV3: Inve 1A **20** (4E **7**)	Admirals Vw. IV2: West 6B **10**	Alexander St. IV9: Avo 6A **16**
Abbey Ct. IV3: Inve 1A **20** (4F **7**)	Admirals Wlk. IV2: West 5B **10**	Alltan Ct. IV2: Cull 3A **10**
Abbotsford Ter. IV3: Inve . . .3B **20** (5F **7**)	Admirals Way IV2: West 5A **10**	Alltan Pk. IV2: Cull 3A **10**
Abertarff Rd. IV2: Inve 5H **7**	Aird Av. IV2: Inve 2H **13**	Alltan Pl. IV2: Cull 3A **10**
Academy St. IV1: Inve 2C **20** (4G **7**)	Alamein Dr. IV2: Inve 5B **8**	Anderson Ct. *IV3: Inve* 3F **7**
IV10: Fort 3F **17**	Alder Pl. IV2: Cull 2A **10**	*(off Madras St.)*
	Aldourie Rd. IV2: Inve 4E **13**	Anderson Dr. IV10: Fort 3F **17**

Anderson St.
    IV3: Inve 1A **20** (2E **7**)
Annfield Rd. IV2: Inve 6H **7**
Anzio Rd. IV2: Inve 5B **8**
Ardbreck Pl. IV2: Inve 5E **13**
Ardconnel St. IV2: Inve 4D **20** (5G **7**)
Ardconnel Ter.
    IV2: Inve 4D **20** (5G **7**)
ARDERSIER 3F **19**
Ardersier Ind. Est. IV2: Ard . . .3G **19**
Ardholm Pl. IV2: Inve 5E **13**
Ardness Pl. IV2: Inve 5E **13**
Ardross Ct. IV3: Inve 5A **20** (6F **7**)
Ardross Pl. IV3: Inve 5A **20** (6F **7**)
Ardross St. IV3: Inve 5A **20** (6F **7**)
Ardross Ter. IV3: Inve 4B **20** (5F **7**)
Ardtower Rd. IV2: West 1G **15**
Argyle Ct. IV2: Inve 6H **7**
Argyle St. IV2: Inve 5D **20** (6G **7**)
Argyle Ter. IV2: Inve 5D **20** (6G **7**)
Ashie Rd. IV2: Inve 4G **13**
Ashton Cres. IV2: Inve 5B **8**
Ashton Rd. IV2: Inve 5B **8**
Ashwood Gro. IV2: Milt L 5E **15**
Aspen Pl. IV2: Cull 2A **10**
Assynt Rd. IV3: Inve 6C **6**
Attadale Rd. IV3: Inve . . .3A **20** (5E **7**)
Auldcastle Rd. IV2: Inve 4H **7**
Aultnaskiach IV2: Inve 1G **13**
Aultnaskiach Av. IV2: Inve 1G **13**
AVOCH .6A **16**

B

Balfour Ct. IV10: Fort 3F **17**
BALLIFEARY 1F **13**
Balliffeary La.
    IV3: Inve 6A **20** (1F **13**)
Balliffeary Rd. IV3: Inve 1E **13**
Balloan Pk. IV2: Inve 3A **14**
Balloan Rd. IV2: Inve 4H **13**
BALLOCH 2D **10**
Balmoral Ter. IV2: Inve 6B **8**
Balnacraig Ct. IV3: Inve 4D **6**
Balnacraig La. IV3: Inve 4E **7**
Balnacraig Rd. IV3: Inve 4D **6**
Balnafettack Cres. IV3: Inve 5B **6**
Balnafettack Pl. IV3: Inve 5B **6**
Balnafettack Rd. IV3: Inve 5B **6**
Balnain St. IV3: Inve 3B **20** (5F **7**)
Balnakyle Rd. IV2: Inve 5E **13**
Balvonie Av. IV2: Inve 1C **14**
Balvonie Brae IV2: Milt L 5F **15**
BALVONIE BRAES 5F **15**
Balvonie Grn. IV2: Milt L 5F **15**
Balvonie Sq. IV2: Milt L 5F **15**
Balvonie St. IV2: Milt L 5F **15**
Balvonie Ter. IV2: Milt L 5F **15**
Bank La. IV1: Inve 3C **20** (5G **7**)
Bank St. IV1: Inve 3B **20** (5F **7**)
Bannatyne's Health Club
    Inverness 1B **14**
Barn Chu. Rd.
    IV2: Ball, Cull, Inve, Smith, Milt C
    . . . . .3F **9**
Barnview IV2: Cull 4A **10**
Baron Taylor's St.
    IV1: Inve 3C **20** (5G **7**)
Beaton's La. IV1: Inve . . .2B **20** (4F **7**)
Beaufort Rd. IV2: Inve 5H **7**
Beech Av. IV2: Inve 2G **13**
Beechwood Bus. Pk. IV2: Inve 6C **8**

Beechwood Bus. Pk. Nth.
    IV2: Inve 6C **8**
Beechwood Ct. IV2: Inve 5B **8**
Beechwood Rd. IV2: Inve 5B **8**
Bellfield Dr. IV1: N Kes 5C **4**
Bellfield Pk. IV2: Inve 6C **20** (1G **13**)
Bellfield Rd. IV1: N Kes 5B **4**
Bellfield Ter.
    IV2: Inve 6C **20** (1G **13**)
Benula Rd. IV3: Inve 1A **20** (3E **7**)
Berneray Ct. IV2: Inve 1A **14**
Birch Ct. IV2: Smith 4A **10**
Birch Pl. IV2: Cull 2A **10**
Birchview Ct. IV2: Insh 2F **15**
Birchwood Brae IV2: Insh 1F **15**
Birchwood Ct. IV2: Insh 2F **15**
Birchwood La. IV2: Insh 1F **15**
Birchwood Pl. IV2: Insh 2F **15**
Birchwood Rd. IV2: Insh 2F **15**
Birchwood Ter. IV2: Insh 2F **15**
Birnie Ter. IV3: Inve 4E **7**
Bishops Pk. IV3: Inve 6A **20** (6F **7**)
Bishops Rd. IV3: Inve 6A **20** (6F **7**)
    IV10: Fort 4E **17**
Bishop's Vw. IV3: Craig D 2A **12**
Black Isle Leisure Cen. 4G **17**
Black Isle Riding Cen. 2C **4**
Black Isle Wildlife & Country Park
    . . . . .1C **4**
BLACKPARK 5A **6**
Blackpark Ter. IV3: Inve 3C **6**
Blackthorn Rd. IV2: Cull 2A **10**
Blackwell Av. IV2: Cull 3B **10**
Blackwell Ct. IV2: Cull 3B **10**
Blackwell Rd. IV2: Cull 3B **10**
Blarmore Av. IV3: Inve 5C **6**
Boarstone Av. IV2: Inve 5D **12**
Boarstone Ct. IV2: Inve 5D **12**
Boarstone Pl. IV2: Inve 5D **12**
BOGALLAN 1A **4**
Borlum Rd. IV2: Inve 4D **12**
Boswell Cres. IV2: Inve 4C **14**
Boswell Pk. IV2: Inve 4C **14**
Boswell Rd. IV2: Inve 3B **14**
Bow Ct. IV1: Inve 3C **20**
Braehead IV9: Avo 6A **16**
Braeside Pk. IV2: Ball 2D **10**
Bramble Cl. IV2: Inve 6H **13**
Branxholme Ter. IV2: Inve 4E **13**
BREASIDE PARK 1D **10**
Bremner Gdns. IV2: Smith 4H **9**
Briargrove Cres. IV2: Insh 2D **14**
Briargrove Dr.
    IV2: Insh, Inve 2D **14**
Briargrove Gdns. IV2: Insh 2D **14**
Briargrove Ter. IV2: Insh 2D **14**
Bridge St. IV1: Inve 4C **20** (5G **7**)
    IV9: Avo 6A **16**
    IV10: Rose 1G **17**
Bridgeview Dr. IV3: Inve 2E **7**
Brinckman Ter. IV2: West 1G **15**
Broadstone Av. IV2: Inve 6H **7**
Broadstone Pk. IV2: Inve 5H **7**
Brookfield IV2: Cull M 4H **11**
Broom Dr. IV2: Inve 3G **13**
Brown St. IV3: Inve 1A **20** (3F **7**)
Bruce Av. IV2: Inve 6E **7**
Bruce Gdns. IV3: Inve 6A **20** (1D **12**)
    IV10: Fort 3F **17**
Bruce Pk. IV3: Inve 6A **20** (6E **7**)
Brude's Hill IV3: Inve 6B **6**
BUGHT 2E **13**
Bught Av. IV3: Inve 2E **13**

Bught Caravan Pk. IV3: Inve 2E **13**
Bught Dr. IV3: Inve 2E **13**
Bught La. IV3: Inve 2E **13**
Bught Rd. IV3: Inve 2E **13**
Burma Ct. IV2: Inve 6B **8**
Burn Brae IV2: West 6H **9**
Burn Brae Av. IV2: West 6H **9**
Burn Brae Cres. IV2: West 6H **9**
Burn Brae Pl. IV2: West 6A **10**
Burn Brae Ter. IV2: West 6H **9**
Burnett Rd. IV1: Inve 1C **20** (4G **7**)
Burn Rd. IV2: Inve 2G **13**
Burnside Dr. IV2: West 5H **9**
By the Bridge IV1: Inve 4C **20**

C

Cairn Ct. IV3: Inve 6C **6**
Caledonian Rd. IV3: Inve 5D **6**
Caledonian Stadium 1H **7**
Cameron Av. IV2: Ball 2D **10**
Cameron Ct. IV2: Smith 5H **9**
Cameron Dr. IV2: Ard 3F **19**
Cameron Rd. IV3: Inve 4E **7**
Cameron Sq. IV3: Inve 4E **7**
Campbelltown IV2: Ard 4F **19**
Canal Rd. IV3: Inve 5C **6**
Canal Ter. IV3: Inve 4D **6**
Canonbury Ter. IV10: Fort 4E **17**
Carlton Bingo
    Inverness 6C **8**
Carlton Ter. IV2: Inve 4A **8**
Carnarc Cres. IV3: Inve 2E **7**
Carn Gorm Ter. IV3: Inve 6C **6**
Carsegate Rd. IV3: Inve 3D **6**
Carsegate Rd. Nth. IV3: Inve 3E **7**
Carsegate Rd. Sth. IV3: Inve 3D **6**
Carse Ind. Est. IV3: Inve 3E **7**
Carse Rd. IV3: Inve 4E **7**
Castlebay Gdns. IV3: Inve 6B **6**
CASTLE HEATHER 4A **14**
Castle Heather Av. IV2: Inve 4A **14**
Castle Heather Cres.
    IV2: Inve 4A **14**
    (not continuous)
Castle Heather Dr. IV2: Inve 4H **13**
Castle Heather Rd. IV2: Inve 3A **14**
Castlehill Ct. IV2: Crad 6E **9**
Castlehill Dr. IV2: Crad 1E **15**
Castlehill Gdns. IV2: Crad 1E **15**
Castlehill Pk. IV2: Crad 1E **15**
Castle Rd. IV2: Inve 4C **20** (5G **7**)
Castle St. IV2: Inve 4C **20** (5G **7**)
    IV10: Fort 3F **17**
Castleton Village
    IV2: Milt L 6E **15**
Castle Wynd IV2: Inve 4C **20** (5G **7**)
Cathedral Sq. IV10: Fort 3F **17**
Cauldeen Rd. IV2: Inve 2H **13**
Caulfield Av. IV2: Crad 6G **9**
Caulfield Gdns. IV2: Crad 6G **9**
Caulfield Pk. IV2: Crad 6G **9**
Caulfield Pl. IV2: Crad 6G **9**
Caulfield Rd.
    IV2: All, Cull . . . . .3H **9** & 1A **10**
    (not continuous)
    IV2: Crad, West 1E **15**
Caulfield Rd. Nth. IV2: Crad 1D **14**
Caulfield Rd. Sth. IV2: West 1F **15**
Caulfield Ter. IV2: Crad 6G **9**
Cavell Gdns. IV2: Inve 6B **20** (6F **7**)
Cawdor Rd. IV2: Inve 5H **7**

Cedarwood Av. IV2: Milt L 5D 14
Cedarwood Cres. IV2: Milt L 5D 14
Cedarwood Dr. IV2: Milt L 5D 14
Cedarwood Gdns.
 IV2: Milt L 5D 14
Celt St. IV3: Inve 3A 20 (5F 7)
Chanonry Cres. IV10: Fort 4G 17
Chanonry Ga. IV10: Fort 3H 17
CHANONRY NESS 4H 17
Chanonry Sailing Club 4F 17
Chapel St. IV1: Inve 2B 20 (4F 7)
Charles St. IV2: Inve 4D 20 (5G 7)
Charleston Ct. IV3: Inve 6C 6
Charleston Pl. IV3: Inve 4D 6
Charleston Rd. IV1: N Kes 5C 4
Charleston Vw. IV3: Inve 1C 12
CHARLESTOWN 5C 4
Chattan Av. IV2: Inve 5C 8
Cherry Pk. IV2: Ball 2C 10
Churchill Rd. IV2: Inve 5B 8
Church La. IV1: Inve 3B 20 (5F 7)
Church Pl. IV10: Rose 1H 17
Church St. IV1: Inve 2B 20 (4F 7)
 IV10: Fort 3F 17
CITADEL 3G 7
Clachan Rd. IV2: Ard 3F 19
Clachnacuddin FC 3E 7
CLACHNAHARRY 3C 6
Clachnaharry Ct. IV3: Inve 4D 6
Clachnaharry Rd.
 IV3: Clac, Del, Inve 4A 6
 (not continuous)
Clava Rd. IV2: Inve 3H 13
Cloverfield Pk. IV2: Inve 2C 14
Cloverfield Rd. IV2: Inve 2C 14
CNOC AN TO'RRA 5A 4
COLDWELL 3B 4
Columba Rd. IV3: Inve 6E 7
Connage Highland Dairy 4F 19
Connel Ct. IV2: Inve 4D 20 (5G 7)
Cook Dr. IV2: Inve 2A 14
Corbett Gdns. IV2: Ard 3F 19
Coronation Pk. IV3: Inve 3E 7
Coronation Rd. IV3: Inve 3E 7
County Cotts. IV2: Culd 6G 13
Courthill Rd. IV10: Rose 2G 17
Cradlehall Bus. Pk. IV2: Crad 6E 9
Cradlehall Ct. IV2: Crad 6F 9
Cradlehall Farm Dr. IV2: Crad 6F 9
Cradlehall Gdns. IV2: Crad 6G 9
Cradlehall Mdws. IV2: Crad 6F 9
Cradlehall Pk. IV2: West 1F 15
Craigard Pl. IV3: Inve 5D 6
Craigard Ter. IV3: Inve 5D 6
Craig Phadrig Hill Fort 5A 6
Craigphadrig Ter. IV3: Inve 1A 20
Craigton Av. IV3: Inve 2E 7
Cranmore Dr. IV2: Smith 5G 9
Crawford Av. IV10: Rose 2G 17
Creag Dhubh Ter. IV3: Inve 6C 6
Croft La. IV3: Inve 3B 6
CROFT NA CREICH 3A 4
Croft Rd. IV3: Inve 4C 6
Cromal Ter. IV2: Ard 1E 19
Cromwell Ct. IV1: Inve 1B 20
Cromwell Ind. Units
 IV1: Inve 3G 7
Cromwell Rd. IV1: Inve 3F 7
Cromwell's Clock Tower 3F 7
CROWN 5H 7
Crown Av. IV2: Inve 5H 7
Crown Cir. IV2: Inve 5H 7
Crown Dr. IV2: Inve 4H 7

Crown Rd. IV2: Inve 3D 20 (5G 7)
Crown St. IV2: Inve 4D 20 (5G 7)
CULCABOCK 1B 14
Culcabock Av. IV2: Inve 1B 14
Culcabock Rd. IV2: Inve 6A 8
Culduthel Av. IV2: Culd, Inve 6E 13
Culduthel Ct. IV2: Inve 4H 13
Culduthel Cres. IV2: Inve 4G 13
Culduthel Gdns. IV2: Inve 1G 13
Culduthel Mains Av. IV2: Inve 6F 13
Culduthel Mains Circ.
 IV2: Inve 6F 13
Culduthel Mains Ct. IV2: Inve 6E 13
Culduthel Mains Cres.
 IV2: Inve 6F 13
Culduthel Mains Gdns.
 IV2: Inve 6F 13
Culduthel Mains Rd. IV2: Inve 6F 13
Culduthel Pk. IV2: Inve 5F 13
Culduthel Pl. IV2: Inve 4G 13
Culduthel Rd.
 IV2: Culd, Inve 5C 20 (6G 7)
Culduthel Smithy IV2: Culd 6G 13
Culduthel Smithy Gdns.
 IV2: Inve 6G 13
Cullaird Rd. IV2: Inve 4F 13
Cullernie Gdns. IV2: Ball 2E 11
Cullernie Rd. IV2: Ball 1D 10
CULLODEN 3A 10
Culloden Academy Community Complex
 . . . . .2B 10
Culloden Battlefield Vis. Cen. . . .6G 11
Culloden Cen. IV2: Cull 3A 10
Culloden Ct. IV2: Cull 3A 10
Culloden Pk. IV2: Cull 2A 10
Culloden Rd. IV2: Cull 1C 10
 IV2: Crad, Insh, Inve, West 1C 14
Culloden Stables IV2: Cull 3B 10
Curves
 Inverness 4H 7
Cuthbert Rd. IV2: Inve 1B 14

D

DALCROSS 2A 18
Dalcross Ind. Est. IV2: Dal 2A 18
Dalmore Pl. IV2: Cull 3A 10
DALNEIGH 6D 6
Dalneigh Cres. IV3: Inve 6E 7
Dalneigh Rd. IV3: Inve 6E 7
Damfield La. IV2: Inve 1H 13
Damfield Rd. IV2: Inve 1H 13
Dan Corbett Gdns. IV3: Inve 3E 7
Darnaway Av. IV2: Inve 6H 7
Darnaway Rd. IV2: Inve 6H 7
Darris Rd. IV2: Inve 5E 13
David Munro Cl. IV2: Inve 6A 8
Daviot Dr. IV2: Inve 2H 13
Davis Sq. IV3: Inve 2A 20
Deans Rd. IV10: Fort 4F 17
Dell, The IV2: Inve 4G 13
Dellness Av. IV2: Inve 2C 14
Dellness Pk. IV2: Inve 2C 14
Dellness Rd. IV2: Inve 2C 14
Dellness Way IV2: Inve 2C 14
Dell Rd. IV2: Inve 2H 13
DELMORE 4A 6
Delnies Rd. IV2: Inve 2G 13
Delnies Rd. IV2: Inve 2G 13
Denny St. IV2: Inve 4D 20 (5G 7)
Deveron St. IV1: Inve 1B 20 (4F 7)
Devlin Cres. IV2: Inve 4E 13

Diriebught Ct. IV2: Inve 5A 8
Diriebught Rd. IV2: Inve 4A 8
Dochfour Dr. IV3: Inve 6E 7
Dock, The IV9: Avo 6A 16
 (off Shore St.)
Dolphin & Seal Cen. 6E 5
Dolphin Trips Avoch 6B 16
Dores Av. IV2: Inve 4E 13
Dores Rd. IV2: Inve 5D 12
Dornie Pl. IV2: Inve 4F 13
Douglas Row IV1: Inve 2B 20 (4F 7)
Doupac Gdns. IV10: Fort 3F 17
Dovecote Pk. IV2: Cull 3B 10
Drakies Av. IV2: Inve 1B 14
Druid Rd. IV2: Inve 2H 13
Druid Temple Courtyard
 IV2: Inve 4A 14
Druid Temple Cres. IV2: Inve 4B 14
Druid Temple Rd. IV2: Inve 4A 14
Druid Temple Way IV2: Inve 4B 14
Druim Av. IV2: Inve 3F 13
Druim Pk. IV2: Inve 3E 13
Drumashie Rd. IV2: Inve 5F 13
Drumblair Cres. IV2: Inve 4D 12
Drumdevan Cres. IV2: Inve 5F 13
Drumdevan Pl. IV2: Inve 5F 13
Drumdevan Rd. IV2: Inve 5F 13
Drumfield Ct. IV2: Inve 5D 12
Drumfield Rd. IV2: Inve 5D 12
Drummond Cir. IV2: Inve 2G 13
Drummond Ct. IV2: Inve 3G 13
Drummond Cres. IV2: Inve 2F 13
Drummond Pl. IV2: Inve 3F 13
Drummond Rd. IV2: Inve 3F 13
Drummond St.
 IV1: Inve 3C 20 (5G 7)
Drumossie Av. IV2: Inve 2B 14
DRUMSMITTAL 2C 4
Drumsmittal Rd. IV1: N Kes 4C 4
Drynie Av. IV2: Inve 2H 13
Drynie Ter. IV2: Inve 2H 13
Duff St. IV3: Inve 3A 20 (5F 7)
Duffy Dr. IV2: Inve 5D 20 (6G 7)
Duke's Vw. IV2: Inve 6H 13
Dunabban Rd.
 IV3: Inve 1A 20 (4E 7)
Dunachton Rd. IV3: Inve 1F 13
Dunain Rd. IV3: Inve 5E 7
Duncraig Ct. IV3: Inve 4A 20 (5F 7)
Duncraig St. IV3: Inve 4A 20 (5F 7)
DW Fitness
 Inverness 4D 8

E

Easter Greengate IV10: Fort 4G 17
EASTER MUCKOVIE 1H 15
Easter Muckovie IV2: West 1G 15
Eastfield Av. IV2: Inve 6B 8
Eastfield Way IV2: Inve 4D 8
Eastgate IV2: Inve 3D 20 (5G 7)
Eastgate Shop. Cen.
 IV2: Inve 3D 20 (5G 7)
E. Mackenzie Pk. IV2: Inve 2B 14
 (not continuous)
East Watergate IV10: Fort 3F 17
Eden Court Theatre 5B 20 (6F 7)
Edgemoor Pk. IV2: Ball 2E 11
Edington Rd. IV2: Inve 2A 14
Elderwood Pl. IV2: Milt L 5E 15
Elm Pk. IV2: Inve 1G 13
Elmwood Av. IV2: Milt L 4D 14

Eriskay Rd. IV2: Inve 1A 14
Erracht Rd. IV2: Inve 4E 13
Errogie Rd. IV2: Inve 5F 13
Esk Rd. IV2: Inve 3H 13
Essich Gdns. IV2: Inve 6E 13
Essich Rd. IV2: Inve 6E 13
Essich Rdbt. IV2: Inve 6E 13
Evan Barron Rd. IV2: Inve 4H 13

F

Factory La. IV9: Avo 6A 16
Factory St. IV1: Inve 1B 20 (4F 7)
Fairfield La. IV3: Inve ...4B 20 (5F 7)
Fairfield Rd.
   IV3: Inve 3A 20 (4D 6)
Fairways Leisure 4H 13
Fairy Glen Nature Reserve 1F 17
Falcon Av. IV2: Inve 2B 14
Falconer Ct. IV3: Inve ...3A 20 (4F 7)
Falcon Gallery IV2: Inve 3D 20
Falcon Sq. IV1: Inve ...3D 20 (5G 7)
Farraline Pk. IV1: Inve ...2C 20 (4G 7)
Feddon Hill IV10: Fort 4D 16
Fergus Ct. IV3: Inve 3A 20 (5F 7)
Fern Pl. IV2: Cull 3B 10
Ferntower Av. IV2: Cull 4A 10
Ferntower Ct. IV2: Cull 4A 10
Ferntower Pl. IV2: Cull 3B 10
Ferry Brae IV1: N Kes 5C 4
Fettes Rd. IV2: Ard 3G 19
Fiery Hillock IV10: Fort 3H 17
Fir Pl. IV2: Cull 2A 10
First Fld. Av. IV1: N Kes 4B 4
Firthview Av. IV3: Inve 4C 6
Firthview Dr. IV3: Inve 4C 6
Firthview Rd. IV3: Inve 3C 6
Fit4Less
   Inverness 4A 8
Fletcher Gdns. IV9: Avo 5A 16
   (off Rosehaugh East Dr.)
Flora MacDonald Monument 4C 20
Forbes Pl. IV2: Smith 4H 9
Forest Dr. IV2: Ball 2E 11
Forester's Way IV3: Craig D ...2A 12
Forge Gym 3E 7
FORTROSE 3F 17
Fortrose & Rosemarkie Golf Course
.........3H 17
Fortrose Caravan Pk. IV10: Fort ...4G 17
Fortrose Cathedral (remains of)
.........4F 17
Fraser Ct. IV2: Cull 3H 9
Fraser St. IV1: Inve ...3C 20 (5G 7)
   IV2: Inve 6C 20 (6G 7)
Friars Bri. IV1: Inve ...2A 20 (4F 7)
   IV3: Inve 2A 20 (4F 7)
Friar's La. IV1: Inve ...2B 20 (4F 7)
Friars' Pl.
   IV3: Inve 2A 20 (4F 7)
Friars Shott IV3: Inve ...2A 20 (4E 7)
Friars St. IV1: Inve ...2B 20 (4F 7)
Fulmar Cres. IV2: Ard 2F 19

G

Galloway Dr. IV2: Cull 3H 9
Gallowhill IV9: Avo 6A 16
Garth Rd. IV2: Inve 4F 13
Gean Pl. IV2: West 6A 10
General Booth Rd. IV3: Inve ...6C 6

General Wade's Military Rd.
   IV2: Inve 3B 14
   (off Old Edinburgh Rd. Sth.)
George St. IV1: Inve ...1B 20 (4G 7)
   IV9: Avo 6A 16
Gilbert Ct. IV3: Inve ...1A 20 (4F 7)
Gilbert St. IV3: Inve ...1A 20 (4F 7)
Gladstone Pl.
   IV3: Inve 3A 20 (5E 7)
GLEBE 2B 20 (4F 7)
Glebe, The IV10: Rose 2G 17
Glebe Cotts. IV2: Torn 6B 18
Glebe St. IV1: Inve ...2B 20 (4F 7)
Glenburn Dr. IV2: Inve 2G 13
Glendoe Ter. IV3: Inve 3E 7
Glendruidh Rd. IV2: Inve 2A 14
Glengarry Rd. IV3: Inve 5C 6
Glenshiel Pl. IV2: Inve 3A 14
Glenurquhart Rd.
   IV3: Inve 6A 20 (2E 13)
Godsman's Brae
   IV2: Inve 6C 20 (6G 7)
Godsman's Wlk.
   IV2: Inve 6C 20 (1G 13)
Golf Vw. Ct. IV2: Inve 4B 14
Golf Vw. Rd. IV3: Inve 2C 12
Golf Vw. Ter. IV3: Inve 1B 12
Gollanhead Av. IV10: Rose ...2H 17
Gordon Ter. IV2: Inve ...5C 20 (6G 7)
Gordonville Rd.
   IV2: Inve 6C 20 (6G 7)
Gowanbrae Cres. IV10: Rose ...2H 17
Gowan's Pl. IV9: Avo 6A 16
Grant Rd. IV2: Ball 2D 10
Grant's Cl. IV1: Inve ...3C 20 (5G 7)
Grant St. IV1: Inve ...1A 20 (3F 7)
   IV3: Inve 1A 20 (3F 7)
Grant Street Pk. 3E 7
Grebe Av. IV2: Inve 2B 14
Green Dr. IV2: Inve 4G 13
Greengates Pl. IV10: Fort ...4G 17
Greenside Av. IV10: Rose 2G 17
Greenwood Ct. IV2: Milt L ...5D 14
Greenwood Dr. IV2: Milt L ...5D 14
Greenwood Gdns.
   IV2: Milt L 5D 14
Greenwood Pl. IV2: Milt L ...5D 14
Greig St. IV3: Inve ...3A 20 (5F 7)
Grigor Dr. IV2: Inve 4E 13
Grigor Gdns. IV2: Inve 4E 13
Groam House Mus. 1H 17
Grove Ter. IV2: Inve ...6C 20 (6G 7)

H

Hamilton St. IV2: Inve ...3D 20 (5G 7)
Harbour Ct. IV3: Inve 2E 7
Harbour Rd. IV1: Inve ...1D 20 (3G 7)
   IV10: Fort 4E 17
Harbour Rd. Rdbt. IV1: Inve ...3H 7
Harris Rd. IV2: Inve 1H 13
Harrowden Rd.
   IV3: Inve 3A 20 (5E 7)
HAUGH 6C 20 (6G 7)
Haugh Ct. IV2: Inve ...6C 20 (6G 7)
Haugh Rd. IV2: Inve ...6C 20 (6G 7)
Hawkhill Rd. IV10: Rose 1H 17
Hawthorn Dr. IV3: Inve 5D 6
Hayfield Av. IV2: Inve 2C 14
Hazel Av. IV2: Cull 2A 10
Heathcote Gdns. IV2: Inve ...1G 13
Heatherley Cres. IV2: Inve ...1G 13

Heather Rd. IV2: Inve 2A 14
Heathmount Rd. IV2: Inve ...6H 7
Heights of Woodside
   IV2: West 6A 10
Henderson Dr. IV1: Inve 2G 7
Henderson Rd. IV1: Inve 3G 7
Heraghty Lodge IV2: Inve 3E 13
Highfield Av. IV2: Inve 5C 6
Highlander Way IV2: Inve 4D 8
HIGHLAND HOSPICE 6B 20 (6F 7)
High St. IV1: Inve ...4C 20 (5G 7)
   IV2: Ard 2F 19
   (not continuous)
   IV3: Clac 3C 6
   IV9: Avo 6A 16
   IV10: Fort 4E 17
   IV10: Rose 1H 17
Hillhead IV2: Ard 1F 19
Hill Pk. IV2: Inve 1G 13
Hill Pl. IV2: Inve ...4D 20 (5G 7)
Hillside Dr. IV2: West 6H 9
Hillside Vs. IV2: Inve 4D 20
Hill St. IV2: Inve ...4D 20 (5G 7)
HILTON 2A 14
Hilton Av. IV2: Inve 2H 13
Hilton Ct. IV2: Inve 3A 14
Hilton Cres. IV2: Inve 2A 14
Hilton Village IV2: Inve 3H 13
HMP Inverness (Porterfield)
   IV2: Inve 5D 20
Holm Av. IV2: Inve 3E 13
Holm Burn Pl. IV2: Inve 5D 12
Holm Dell Av. IV2: Inve 5D 12
Holm Dell Ct. IV2: Inve 6E 13
Holm Dell Dr. IV2: Inve 6E 13
Holm Dell Gdns.
   IV2: Inve 6E 13
Holm Dell Pk. IV2: Inve 6E 13
Holm Dell Pl. IV2: Inve 6E 13
Holm Dell Rd. IV2: Inve 6E 13
Holme's Cl. IV10: Rose 1H 17
Holm Farm Rd. IV2: Inve 6G 13
Holm Mills Rd. IV2: Inve 3E 13
Holm Pk. IV2: Inve 5D 12
Holm Rd. IV2: Inve 5D 12
Holm Rdbt. IV2: Inve 5C 12
Huntly Ct. IV3: Inve ...3A 20 (4F 7)
Huntly Pl. IV3: Inve ...2A 20 (4F 7)
Huntly St. IV3: Inve ...2A 20 (4F 7)
Huntly Ter. IV3: Inve 4B 20

I

Icesportinverness 2E 13
India St. IV3: Inve 3F 7
Inglis St. IV1: Inve ...3D 20 (5G 7)
Innes St. IV1: Inve ...1B 20 (4F 7)
INSHES 1F 15
Inshes Brae IV2: West 1F 15
Inshes Ct. IV2: Insh 1F 15
Inshes Cres. IV2: Inve 1B 14
Inshes M. IV2: Inve 2C 14
   (not continuous)
Inshes Retail Pk. IV2: Inve 1C 14
Inshes Rd. IV2: Inve 2C 14
Inshes Vw. IV2: West 1E 15
Interchange Retail Pk.
   IV2: Inve 4B 8
INVERNESS 3C 20 (5G 7)
INVERNESS AIRPORT 3B 18
Inverness & District Indoor Bowling Club
.........4H 13

Inverness Caledonian Thistle FC
. . . . .1H 7
Inverness Castle 4C 20 (5G 7)
Inverness Cathedral 5B 20 (6F 7)
Inverness College
  Longman Campus 1D 20 (3G 7)
  Midmills Campus 5H 7
  Scottish School of Forestry . . .3E 11
Inverness Crematorium
  IV3: Inve 2A 12
Inverness Floral Hall 2E 13
Inverness Golf Course 6B 8
Inverness Leisure 2E 13
Inverness Museum & Art Gallery
. . . . .4C 20 (5G 7)
Inverness Retail & Bus. Pk.
  IV2: Inve 4E 9
Inverness Station (Rail) . . .3D 20 (4G 7)
Inverness Tennis & Squash Club
. . . . .6A 20
Iona Rd. IV3: Inve 4D 6
Island Bank Rd.
  IV2: Inve 6C 20 (3F 13)
Islands Ct. IV2: Inve 1G 13
Islay Rd. IV2: Inve 6A 8

J

Jacobite Cruises 2D 12
Jamaica Gdns. IV3: Inve 3F 7
Jamaica St. IV3: Inve 3F 7
James Pringle Weavers 3E 13
James St. IV9: Avo 6A 16
Johnston Pl. IV2: Inve 3H 13
John St. IV9: Avo 6A 16
Juniper Gdns. IV2: Inve 6H 13
Justice of the Peace Court
  Inverness 4C 20 (5G 7)

K

Kennedy Dr. IV3: Inve 3C 6
Kenneth Pl. IV2: Smith 5H 9
Kenneth St. IV3: Inve 3A 20 (5F 7)
Keppoch Rd. IV2: Cull 3A 10
Kessock Av. IV3: Inve 2E 7
Kessock Bri. IV1: Inve 6F 5
Kessock Ct. Nth. IV3: Inve 2E 7
Kessock Rd. IV3: Inve 1E 7
Kestrel Pl. IV2: Inve 3B 14
Kildonan Cres. IV2: Inve 2H 13
KILMUIR 2H 5
Kilmuir Ct. IV3: Inve 3E 7
Kilmuir Rd. IV3: Inve 3E 7
Kilvean Rd. IV3: Inve 3A 12
Kincraig Ter. IV3: Inve 4C 6
Kincurdy Dr. IV10: Rose 1H 17
King Brude Gdns. IV3: Inve 4D 6
King Brude Rd. IV3: Inve 5C 6
King Brude Ter. IV3: Inve 4D 6
King Duncan's Gdns.
  IV2: Inve 5B 8
King Duncan's Rd. IV2: Inve 4B 8
Kingsmills Gdns. IV2: Inve 6A 8
Kingsmills Leisure Club 6A 8
Kingsmills Pk. IV2: Inve 6H 7
Kingsmills Rd. IV2: Inve 5H 7
King St. IV3: Inve 3A 20 (5F 7)
Kingsview Ter. IV3: Inve 5B 6
KINMYLIES 6B 6
Kinmylies Way IV3: Inve 6C 6

Kintail Ct. IV2: Inve 3H 13
Kintail Cres. IV2: Inve 3H 13
Kirkwall Brae IV3: Inve 6B 6
Knockbain Rd. IV1: Drum 4C 4
Knockmuir Vw. IV9: Avo 5A 16
Knocknagael IV2: Inve 6H 13
Knocknagael Boar Stone 5A 20

L

Ladies Wlk.
  IV2: Inve 6B 20 (1F 13)
Lady Hill Vw. IV9: Avo 5A 16
Laggan Rd. IV2: Inve 4F 13
Lamont Bldgs. IV2: Inve 5C 20
Larch Pl. IV2: Cull 2A 10
Larchwood Cres. IV2: Milt L 5E 15
Larchwood Dr. IV2: Milt L 4E 15
Laurel Av. IV3: Inve 6E 7
Laurel Cotts. IV3: Inve 6D 6
Laurel Pl. IV3: Inve 6E 7
Lawers Way IV3: Inve 6C 6
LEACHKIN 1A 12
Leachkin Av. IV3: Inve 5C 6
Leachkin Brae
  IV3: Inve, Leac 6A 6
Leachkin Dr. IV3: Inve 5C 6
Leachkin Pk. IV3: Inve 5C 6
Leachkin Rd. IV3: Inve 1A 12
Leachkin Ter. IV3: Inve 5C 6
LEANACH 5H 11
Leanach Ct. IV2: West 1H 15
Leanach Gdns. IV2: West 1H 15
Lerwick Cres. IV3: Inve 1B 12
Leys Dr. IV2: Inve 6H 7
Leys Pk. IV2: Inve 6H 7
Leys Rdbt. IV2: Inve 6G 13
Leyton Dr. IV2: Inve 3H 13
Lifeboat Station
  Kessock 6F 5
Lilac Gro. IV3: Inve 5D 6
Limetree Av. IV3: Inve 5D 6
Lindsay Av. IV3: Inve 6A 20 (1E 13)
Lit. Cullernie Pk. IV2: Ball 2D 10
Lochalsh Ct. IV3: Inve 1A 20
Lochalsh Rd. IV3: Inve . . .2A 20 (5E 7)
LOCHARDIL 4F 13
Lochardil Pl. IV2: Inve 4E 13
Lochardil Rd. IV2: Inve 4F 13
Lochiel Gdns. IV2: Inve 2A 14
Lochiel Rd. IV2: Inve 1A 14
Loch Lann Av. IV2: Cull 4A 10
Loch Lann Ct. IV2: Cull 4A 10
Loch Lann Cres. IV2: Cull 4A 10
Loch Lann Rd. IV2: Cull 4A 10
Loch Lann Ter. IV2: Cull 4A 10
Loch Ness Golf Course 4H 13
Lochy Rd. IV2: Inve 4G 13
Lodge Av. IV2: Inve 3G 13
Lodge Pk. IV2: Inve 3G 13
Lodge Rd. IV2: Inve 3G 13
Lombard St. IV1: Inve 3C 20 (5G 7)
Lomond Gdns. IV3: Inve 6B 6
Lomond Way IV3: Inve 6B 6
Longman Caravan Pk.
  IV1: Inve 1H 7
Longman Dr. IV1: Inve 2F 7
            (not continuous)
Longman Ind. Est.
  IV1: Inve 1D 20 (2G 7)
            (not continuous)
Longman Rd. IV1: Inve 1B 20 (4G 7)

Longman Rdbt. IV1: Inve 2H 7
Long Rd. IV9: Avo 6A 16
Lotland Ind. Est. IV1: Inve 3G 7
Lotland Pl. IV1: Inve 3G 7
Lotland St. IV1: Inve 2F 7
Lovat Rd. IV2: Inve 5H 7
LOWER DRUMMOND 2G 13
Lwr. Kessock St. IV3: Inve 3F 7
LOWER SLACKBUIE 6H 13
Lower Wards IV10: Fort 3F 17
Low St. IV3: Clac 2C 6
Lumsden Gdns. IV10: Fort 4G 17

M

Macdonald Ct. IV2: Cull 3H 9
Macdonald St.
  IV2: Inve 6C 20 (6G 7)
Macdowall Ct. IV10: Fort 3F 17
Macewen Ct. IV2: Inve 5A 8
Macewen Dr. IV2: Inve 6H 7
Macgillivary Ct. IV2: Cull 3H 9
Macinnes Pl. IV1: Inve 1B 20
Mackay Rd. IV2: Inve 3H 13
Mackay Ter. IV9: Avo 6A 16
Mackeddie Dr. IV10: Fort 3F 17
Mackenzie Pk. Gdns.
  IV2: Inve 2B 14
Mackenzie Pl. IV9: Avo 6A 16
Mackenzie Rd. IV2: Inve 2A 14
Mackenzie Ter. IV10: Rose 2H 17
Mackintosh Pl. IV2: Inve 4B 8
Mackintosh Rd. IV2: Inve 5B 8
Maclean Ct. IV2: Cull 3H 9
Maclennan Cres. IV3: Inve 3F 7
Maclennan Gdns. IV3: Inve 3F 7
Macleod Rd. IV2: Ball 2D 10
Madras Ct. *IV3: Inve* 3F 7
          (off Madras St.)
Madras St. IV3: Inve 3F 7
Main St. IV1: N Kes 6D 4
Mamore Ter. IV3: Inve 6C 6
Manse Brae IV10: Rose 2G 17
Manse Dr. IV9: Avo 6A 16
Manse Pl. IV1: Inve 2B 20 (4G 7)
Manse Rd. IV2: Ard 3F 19
Maple Dr. IV3: Inve 5D 6
Marchburn Ct. IV1: N Kes 4B 4
Margaret St. IV1: Inve 2C 20 (4G 7)
  IV9: Avo 6A 16
Marine Pk. IV1: N Kes 5C 4
Marine Ter. IV10: Rose 1H 17
Market Brae IV2: Inve 3D 20 (5G 7)
Market Cl. IV1: Inve 3C 20
Market Hall IV1: Inve 3C 20
Mary Ann Ct. IV3: Inve 4B 20 (5F 7)
Maryfield Gdns. IV2: Inve 5A 8
Mason Rd. IV2: Inve 3A 14
Maxwell Dr. IV3: Inve 6E 7
May Ct. IV3: Inve 4B 20 (5F 7)
Mayfield Rd.
  IV2: Inve 5D 20 (6G 7)
May Ter. IV3: Inve 4B 20
Meadowbank IV1: N Kes 4C 4
Meadowfield Av. IV2: Inve 2D 14
Meadowfield Pk. IV2: Inve 2C 14
Meadow Rd. IV2: Ball 1E 11
Mealmarket Cl. IV1: Inve 3D 20
MERKINCH 4F 7
Merlewood Rd. IV2: Inve 3G 13
Merlin Cres. IV2: Inve 2B 14

Midmills Rd. IV2: Inve 5H 7
Mid St. IV3: Clac 2C 6
Miers Av. IV2: Inve 1B 14
Mile End Pl. IV3: Inve 1C 12
Millbank IV1: N Kes 4C 4
MILLBURN **4A 8**
Millburn Ct. IV2: Inve 4A 8
Millburn Pl. IV2: Inve 4A 8
Millburn Rd. IV2: Inve 3D 20 (5G 7)
Millburn Rdbt. IV2: Inve 4B 8
Millburn Sq. IV2: Inve 4A 8
Mill Ct. IV3: Inve 2E 7
Mill Cres. IV1: N Kes 5B 4
Miller Gdns. IV2: Inve 3C 14
Miller Rd. IV2: Inve 3B 14
Miller's Arch IV10: Rose 1H 17
Miller St. IV2: Inve 3B 14
Millerton Av. IV3: Inve 1C 12
Millerton Vw. IV3: Inve 1C 12
Mill Rd. IV10: Rose 1H 17
Milton Cres. IV2: Inve 2A 14
MILTON OF CULLODEN **1G 9**
MILTON OF CULLODEN SOUTH . . .**2A 10**
MILTON OF LEYS **5D 14**
Mitchell's La. IV2: Inve 5D 20 (6G 7)
Montague Row
  IV3: Inve 4A 20 (5F 7)
Moray Dr. IV2: Ball 2E 11
Moray Pk. IV2: Inve 6C 20
Moray Pk. Av. IV2: Cull 2C 10
Moray Pk. Cres. IV2: Cull 3B 10
Moray Pk. Gdns. IV2: Cull 3C 10
Moray Pk. La. IV2: Cull 3C 10
Moray Pk. Pl. IV2: Cull 3B 10
Moray Pk. Ter. IV2: Cull 3C 10
Moray Pk. Wynd IV2: Cull 3C 10
Morning Fld. Dr.
  IV2: Culd, Inve 6G 13
Morning Fld. Pl. IV2: Inve 6H 13
Morning Fld. Rd. IV2: Inve 6H 13
Morven Rd. IV2: Inve 4F 13
Morvich Way IV2: Inve 3H 13
Moy Ter. IV2: Inve 4G 13
Muirfield Ct. IV2: Inve 1H 13
Muirfield Gdns. IV2: Inve 1H 13
Muirfield La. IV2: Inve 1H 13
Muirfield Pk. IV2: Inve 1H 13
Muirfield Rd. IV2: Inve 1H 13
MUIRTOWN **4A 6**
Muirtown Ho. IV3: Inve 4C 6
Muirtown St.
  IV3: Inve 2A 20 (5F 7)
Muirtown Ter. IV3: Inve 3D 6
Munro Ter. IV10: Rose 2H 17
Murray Pl. IV2: Inve 6C 20
  IV2: Smith 4H 9
Murray Rd. IV2: Smith 5H 9
Murray Ter. IV2: Smith 5A 10
Myrtlefield La. IV2: West 6A 10
Myrtletown Pk. IV2: West 6H 9

N

Nairn Rd. IV2: Ard 4F 19
Neil Gunn Cres. IV2: Inve 3B 14
Nelson St. IV3: Inve 1A 20 (3F 7)
Ness Bank IV2: Inve 6B 20 (6F 7)
Ness Ct. IV2: Inve 5C 20 (6G 7)
Ness Pl. IV2: Inve 5C 20 (6G 7)
Ness Rd. IV10: Fort 3F 17
Ness Rd. E. IV10: Fort 3H 17
Ness Ter. IV2: Inve 6C 20

Ness Wlk. IV3: Inve 4B 20 (5F 7)
Ness Way IV10: Fort 4H 17
NETHER CRAIGTON **5F 5**
Nevis Pk. IV3: Inve 5B 6
NEW CRAIGS PSYCHIATRIC HOSPITAL
  . . . .**1B 12**
New Market IV1: Inve . . .3C 20 (5G 7)
Nth. Church Pl.
  IV1: Inve 2B 20 (4F 7)
NORTH KESSOCK **6D 4**

O

Oak Av. IV2: Inve 3G 13
Oakdene Ct. IV2: Cull 3B 10
Oakleigh Rd. IV1: N Kes 5D 4
Oakwood Pl. IV2: Milt L 5E 15
Oich Ter. IV2: Inve 4G 13
Old Craigton Rd. IV1: N Kes 6E 5
Old Edinburgh Ct. IV2: Inve 1H 13
Old Edinburgh Rd.
  IV2: Inve 5C 20 (6G 7)
  (not continuous)
Old Edinburgh Rd. Sth.
  IV2: Inve, Milt L 3B 14
Old Mill IV1: Char 5B 4
Old Mill La. IV2: Inve 1A 14
Old Mill Rd. IV2: Inve 6H 7
  IV9: Avo 6A 16
Old Perth Rd. IV2: Inve 4B 8
Old School Pl. IV3: Inve 3E 7
Old Steading Rd.
  IV3: Inve 6C 6
Oldtown Pl. IV2: Inve 3A 14
Oldtown Rd. IV2: Inve 3H 13
Orchard, The IV10: Fort 4H 17
  (Ness Way)
  IV10: Fort 3E 17
  (Station Cres.)
Orchard Pk. IV2: Crad 6F 9
Orchid Av. IV2: Inve 6H 13
Ord Hill Hill Fort **3F 5**
Ord Ter. IV2: Inve 3E 7
Ormond Dr. IV2: Ball 2E 11
Ormus Ind. Units IV1: Inve 3G 7
Otium Health & Leisure Club **4B 8**
Overton Av. IV3: Inve 3B 6

P

Park Rd. IV3: Inve 6A 20 (6E 7)
Park St. IV9: Avo 6A 16
Paton St. IV2: Inve 6C 20 (6G 7)
Perceval Rd.
  IV3: Inve 3A 20 (5F 7)
Pict Av. IV3: Inve 4D 6
Pine Dr. IV2: Inve 3G 13
Pinewood Ct. IV2: Milt L 5E 15
Pinewood Dr. IV2: Milt L 5E 15
Pinewood Pl. IV2: Milt L 5F 15
Planefield Rd.
  IV3: Inve 4A 20 (5F 7)
Platcock Wynd IV10: Fort 3F 17
Playzone **1C 14**
Point Rd. IV1: N Kes 6E 5
Porterfield Bank
  IV2: Inve 5D 20 (6G 7)
Porterfield Rd.
  IV2: Inve 5D 20 (6G 7)
Portland Pl. IV1: Inve 1B 20 (4F 7)
Portree Ter. IV3: Inve 6B 6

Post Office Av.
  IV1: Inve 3C 20 (5G 7)
Precincts Rd. IV10: Fort 4E 17
Primrose Hill IV2: Inve 6H 13
Provost Smith Cres.
  IV2: Inve 3B 14
Provost Smith Way IV2: Inve 3B 14
Pumpgate Ct. IV3: Inve 3E 7
Pumpgate St. IV3: Inve 3F 7

Q

Quayside Ct. IV3: Inve 2E 7
Queensgate IV1: Inve . . .3C 20 (5G 7)
Queensgate Arc.
  IV1: Inve 3C 20
Queen St. IV3: Inve 3A 20 (5F 7)

R

Raasay Rd. IV2: Inve 1H 13
Raigmore Av. IV2: Inve 6B 8
Raigmore Gdns. IV2: Inve 6B 8
RAIGMORE HOSPITAL **6C 8**
Raigmore Interchange
  IV2: Inve 4C 8
Railway Ter. IV1: Inve . . .2C 20 (4G 7)
Raining's Stairs IV1: Inve 4D 20
Rangemore Rd.
  IV3: Inve 4A 20 (5E 7)
Reaybank Rd. IV2: Ard 3F 19
Reay St. IV2: Inve 4D 20 (5G 7)
Redburn Av. IV2: Cull 4B 10
Redwood Av. IV2: Milt L 6D 14
Redwood Ct. IV2: Milt L 6E 15
Redwood Cres. IV2: Milt L 6D 14
RESAURIE **6G 9**
Rhine Dr. IV2: Inve 5B 8
Richmond Ter. IV3: Inve 3A 20
River Ho. IV3: Inve 4B 20 (5F 7)
Riverside Ct. IV2: Inve 3F 13
Riverside Gdns.
  IV3: Inve 6B 20 (6F 7)
Riverside St. IV1: Inve 1A 20 (4F 7)
River Vw. IV1: Inve 1B 20 (4F 7)
RNI COMMUNITY HOSPITAL
  . . . .**6A 20 (1F 13)**
Rodger Cl. IV10: Fort 3F 17
Rodger Ct. IV10: Fort 3F 17
Roller Bowl **5G 13**
Rosebery Pl. IV2: Inve 6C 20
Rosedene Ct. IV2: Inve 2F 13
Rosehaugh Cres. IV9: Avo 6A 16
Rosehaugh East Dr. IV9: Avo 6A 16
Rosehaugh High Dr.
  IV9: Avo 5A 16
Rosehaugh Rd. IV3: Inve 2E 7
ROSEMARKIE **1H 17**
Rosemarkie Caravan Site
  IV10: Rose 3H 17
Rosemarkie Rd.
  IV10: Fort, Rose 3F 17
Rose Pl. *IV9: Avo* *6A 16*
  (off Rose St.)
Rose St. IV1: Inve 2C 20 (4G 7)
  IV9: Avo 6A 16
  IV10: Fort 4F 17
Rose St. Rdbt.
  IV1: Inve 1C 20 (4G 7)
Ross Av. IV3: Inve 3A 20 (5E 7)
Ross Ct. IV2: Inve 1H 13

Ross Cres. IV10: Fort 3G 17
Rossie Lodge IV2: Inve 3E 13
Round Ho. Av. IV1: N Kes 4B 4
Round Ho. Ct. IV1: N Kes 4B 4
Rowan Ct. IV2: Smith 5G 9
Rowan Gro. IV2: Smith 5H 9
Rowan Rd. IV3: Inve 5D 6
Rowan Way IV2: Smith 5H 9
Royal Ness Ct.
    IV3: Inve 6A 20 (6F 7)
Ruthven Rd. IV2: Inve 4G 13
Ryebank IV10: Rose 2H 17
Ryebank Ct. IV10: Rose 2H 17

S

St Andrew Dr. IV3: Inve 6D 6
St Andrew's Wlk.
    IV10: Fort 4E 17
St Fergus Dr. IV3: Inve 6D 6
St Francis Gdns. IV3: Inve 6D 6
St John's Av. IV3: Inve 6D 6
St Margaret's Rd. IV3: Inve 6D 6
St Mary's Av. IV3: Inve 6E 7
St Mungo Rd. IV3: Inve 6D 6
St Ninian Dr. IV3: Inve 6D 6
St Valery Av. IV3: Inve 6D 6
Sandalwood Av. IV2: Milt L 5C 14
Sandalwood Cres.
    IV2: Milt L 5D 14
Sandalwood Dr. IV2: Milt L 4D 14
School Brae IV9: Avo 6A 16
School La.
    IV1: Inve 3C 20 (4G 7)
School Pl. IV2: Ard 3F 19
SCORGUIE **4C 6**
Scorguie Av. IV3: Inve 4C 6
Scorguie Ct. IV3: Inve 4C 6
Scorguie Dr. IV3: Inve 4C 6
Scorguie Gdns. IV3: Inve 4C 6
Scorguie Pl. IV3: Inve 4C 6
Scorguie Rd. IV3: Inve 3C 6
Scorguie Ter. IV3: Inve 4C 6
Scottish Kiltmaker Cen. . . .**4B 20 (5F 7)**
Seafield Rd. IV1: Inve 3H 7
Seaforth Av. IV2: Ard 3F 19
Seaforth Dr. IV10: Fort 3G 17
Sheriff Court
    Inverness . . . .**4C 20 (5G 7)**
Shoe La. IV3: Inve 1A 20 (4F 7)
Shore St. IV1: Inve 1B 20 (4F 7)
    IV9: Avo 6A 16
Shore St. Rdbt.
    IV1: Inve 1B 20 (4F 7)
Sicily Rd. IV2: Inve 5A 8
Simpson's La. IV3: Inve . . .1A 20 (4F 7)
Sinclair Pk. IV2: Smith 4H 9
Sinclair Ter. IV2: Smith 4H 9
Sir Walter Scott Dr.
    IV2: Cas H 4H 13
Skinner Ct. IV3: Inve 1A 20 (4E 7)
Slackbuie Av. IV2: Inve 4G 13
Slackbuie Cres. IV2: Inve 5G 13
Slackbuie Farm Rd.
    IV2: Culd, Inve 6G 13
Slackbuie Pk. M. IV2: Inve 5H 13
Slackbuie Rdbt. IV2: Inve 5H 13
Slackbuie Way IV2: Cas H 5H 13
Smith Av. IV3: Inve 6A 20 (6E 7)
SMITHTON **4H 9**
Smithton Ind. Est.
    IV2: Smith 4A 10

Smithton Pk. IV2: Smith 5H 9
Smithton Rd. IV2: Smith 5H 9
Smithton Vs. IV2: Smith 4H 9
Somme Cres. IV2: Inve 5B 8
Souter Dr. IV2: Inve 5D 12
SOUTH KESSOCK **2E 7**
Southside Pl. IV2: Inve 6H 7
Southside Rd.
    IV2: Inve 6D 20 (1G 13)
Spectrum Centre, The **2C 20**
Springfield Ct. IV3: Inve 1F 13
Springfield Gdns. IV3: Inve 1F 13
Stadium Bus. Cen.
    IV1: Inve 1G 7
Stadium Rd. IV1: Inve 1G 7
Station Cres. IV10: Fort 3E 17
Station Dr. IV2: Ard 3F 19
Station Rd. IV2: Ard 3F 19
    IV9: Avo 6A 16
    IV10: Fort 3F 17
Station Sq. IV1: Inve 3C 20 (5G 7)
    IV10: Fort 3F 17
Stephen's Brae
    IV2: Inve 3D 20 (5H 7)
Stephens St. IV2: Inve 5H 7
Stevenson Rd. IV2: Inve 3B 14
Stewart Ct. IV2: Cull 3A 10
Stoneyfield IV2: Inve 4D 8
Stoneyfield Bus. Pk.
    IV2: Inve 4D 8
Stornoway Dr. IV3: Inve 1B 12
Strath Av. IV2: Inve 4E 13
Stratherrick Gdns.
    IV2: Inve 4E 13
Stratherrick Pk. IV2: Inve 3F 13
Stratherrick Rd. IV2: Inve 5E 13
Stratton Rd. IV2: Inve 5C 8
Strothers La.
    IV1: Inve 3C 20 (5G 7)
Stuart Av. IV2: Ard 4F 19
Stuarton IV2: Ard 3F 19
    (off Stuart St.)
Stuart Pl. IV2: Ard 3F 19
Stuart St. IV2: Ard 2F 19
Suilven Way IV3: Inve 6C 6
Sunnybank Av. IV2: Inve 1G 13
Sunnybank Rd. IV2: Inve 1G 13
Swan La. IV3: Inve 2A 20 (4F 7)
Swanston Av. IV3: Inve 3C 6
Sycamore Cres. IV2: Inve 1B 14

T

Tannery Ct. IV3: Inve 2E 7
Tap La. IV3: Inve 1A 20 (4F 7)
Tarbert Pl. IV3: Inve 6B 6
Tavern La. IV10: Fort 3F 17
Teal Av. IV2: Inve 2B 14
Telford Av. IV3: Inve 1A 20 (3E 7)
Telford Ct. IV3: Inve 4E 7
Telford Gdns. IV3: Inve 5E 7
Telford Rd.
    IV3: Inve 1A 20 (4E 7)
Telford St. IV3: Inve 2A 20 (4D 6)
Telford St. Rdbt.
    IV3: Inve 2A 20 (4E 7)
Temple Cres. IV2: Inve 2H 13
Tern Av. IV2: Inve 3A 14
The . . . .
    Names prefixed with 'The' for
    example 'The Dell' are indexed under
    the main name such as 'Dell, The'

Thistle Rd. IV2: Inve 1B 14
Thornbush Rd. IV3: Inve 3E 7
Tobermory Pl. IV3: Inve 1B 12
Tobruk Rd. IV2: Inve 6A 8
Toll Rd. IV9: Avo 6A 16
Tomatin Rd. IV2: Inve 2H 13
Tomnahurich St.
    IV3: Inve 5A 20 (6F 7)
Torbreck Rd. IV2: Inve 5F 13
TORNAGRAIN **6B 18**
Torness Rd. IV2: Inve 4E 13
Torris Rd. IV2: Ball 2D 10
TORVEAN **2C 12**
Torvean Av. IV3: Inve 2E 13
Torvean Caravan Pk.
    IV3: Inve 2D 12
Torvean Municipal Golf Course . . .**2D 12**
Tourist Info. Cen.
    Daviot Wood **6G 15**
    Inverness . . . .**4C 20 (5G 7)**
    North Kessock **6D 4**
Tower Brae Nth.
    IV2: Smith, West 5G 9
Tower Brae Sth. IV2: West 6H 9
Tower Ct. IV2: West 1H 15
Tower Gdns. IV2: West 1H 15
Towerhill Av. IV2: Crad 6G 9
Towerhill Cl. IV2: Crad 6G 9
Towerhill Cres. IV2: Crad 6H 9
Towerhill Dr. IV2: Crad 6G 9
Towerhill Gdns. IV2: Crad 6G 9
Towerhill Pl. IV2: Crad 6H 9
Towerhill Rd. IV2: Crad 1G 15
Tower Rd.
    IV2: Crad, Cull, Smith, West 4A 10
Trafford Av. IV3: Inve 4D 6
Trentham Ct. IV2: West 6H 9
Trentham Dr. IV2: West 1H 15
Tullochs Bldgs. IV2: Inve 4D 20

U

Uist Rd. IV2: Inve 1H 13
Underwood Pl. IV2: Ball 2D 10
Union Rd. IV2: Inve 5H 7
Union St. IV1: Inve 3C 20 (5G 7)
    IV10: Fort 3F 17
UPPER CRAIGTON **5E 5**
Up. Cullernie Ct. IV2: Ball 1D 10
Up. Cullernie Pl. IV2: Ball 1D 10
UPPER DRUMMOND **3G 13**
Up. Kessock St.
    IV3: Inve 1A 20 (4F 7)
    (not continuous)
UPPER SLACKBUIE **6H 13**

V

Victoria Dr. IV2: Inve 5H 7
Victoria La. IV2: Inve 4H 7
Victoria Ter. IV2: Inve 4H 7
Viewfield Rd. IV2: Inve 6A 8
VIEWHILL **3E 11**
Viewhill Ga. IV2: Inve 5C 20 (6G 7)
Viewmount Brae
    IV2: West 6A 10
View Pl. IV2: Inve 5C 20 (6G 7)
Visit Scotland Info. Cen.
    Daviot Wood **6G 15**
    Inverness . . . .**4C 20 (5G 7)**
    North Kessock **6D 4**

Vue Cinema
Inverness **4D 8**

W

Wade Rd. IV2: Inve 2A **14**
Wade's Circ. IV2: Inve 4C **10**
Wades Rdbt. IV2: Inve 3B **14**
Walker Cres. IV2: Cull 3H **9**
Walker Pl. IV1: Inve 1C **20** (3G **7**)
Walker Pl. Ind. Units
   IV1: Inve 1C **20** (3G **7**)
Walker Rd. IV1: Inve 1C **20** (3G **7**)
Wallace Pl. IV2: Cull 3A **10**
Warrand Rd. IV3: Inve 1F **13**
Waterfurrows IV10: Fort 3F **17**
Waterloo Pl. IV1: Inve 1B **20** (4F **7**)
Wellingtonia Ct. IV3: Inve 1F **13**
Well Rd. IV10: Rose 1H **17**
Wells Ct. IV3: Inve 2A **20** (4E **7**)
Wellside Av. IV2: Ball 1D **10**
Wellside Gdns. IV2: Ball 1D **10**
Wellside La. IV2: Ball 1D **10**
Wellside Pl. IV2: Ball 1D **10**
Wellside Rd. IV2: Ball 1D **10**
Wells St. IV3: Inve 2A **20** (4F **7**)
Westend Dr. IV2: Ard 3F **19**
Wester Greengates
   IV10: Fort 4G **17**

Wester Inshes Ct. IV2: Inve 3C **14**
Wester Inshes Cres.
   IV2: Inve 2C **14**
Wester Inshes Dr. IV2: Inve 2C **14**
Wester Inshes Gdns.
   IV2: Inve 2C **14**
Wester Inshes Pk. IV2: Inve 2C **14**
Wester Inshes Pl. IV2: Inve 2D **14**
Wester Links IV10: Fort 4H **17**
Westfield Av. IV2: West 6A **10**
Westfield Brae IV2: West 6B **10**
Westfield Dr. IV2: West 6B **10**
Westfield La. IV2: West 6A **10**
Westfield Wlk. IV2: West 6A **10**
Westfield Way IV2: West 6A **10**
W. Heather Gdns. IV2: Inve 4H **13**
W. Heather Rd. IV2: Inve 5G **13**
WESTHILL **6H 9**
W. Mackenzie Pk. IV2: Inve 2B **14**
Whinpark IV3: Inve 5D **6**
Willow Av. IV2: Inve 6H **13**
Wimberley Way IV2: Inve 5A **8**
Woodend Rd. IV2: Ball 2E **11**
Woodgrove Ct. IV2: Inve 2C **14**
Woodgrove Cres. IV2: Inve 1C **14**
Woodgrove Dr. IV2: Inve 2C **14**
Woodgrove Gdns. IV2: Inve 2C **14**
Woodgrove Pl. IV2: Inve 2C **14**
Woodlands Av. IV2: West 5A **10**
Woodlands Cl. IV2: West 5A **10**

Woodlands Ct. IV2: Insh 2F **15**
Woodlands Cres. IV2: West 5A **10**
Woodlands Dr. IV2: West 6H **9**
Woodlands Gro. IV2: West 6A **10**
Woodlands Pk. IV2: West 5A **10**
Woodlands Pl. IV2: Insh 2F **15**
Woodlands Ter. IV2: Insh 2F **15**
Woodlands Vw. IV2: Insh 2F **15**
Woodlands Wlk. IV2: West 5H **9**
Woodlands Way IV2: West 6A **10**
Woodside Brae IV2: West 6A **10**
Woodside Ct. IV2: West 6A **10**
Woodside Cres. IV3: Inve 3C **6**
Woodside Farm Dr.
   IV2: West 5A **10**
Woodside Gdns. IV2: West 6A **10**
Woodside Pk. IV2: West 6A **10**
Woodside Pl. IV2: West 6A **10**
Woodside Ter. IV2: Inve 6B **8**
Woodside Village IV2: West 6A **10**
Wyvis Dr. IV2: Ball 2E **11**
Wyvis Pl. IV3: Inve 3E **7**

Y

YORK DAY HOSPITAL *6A 20*
   (within RNI Community Hospital)
Young Ct. IV10: Rose 2H **17**
Young St. IV3: Inve 4B **20** (5F **7**)